THE
SCHOLARS'
LITTLE MANUAL

OF

Useful Knowledge.

BY

THOMAS CARPENTER,

Author of "The Scholar's Spelling Assistant, School Speaker, &c. &c."

LONDON:

PUBLISHED BY N. MEAD, 93, WHITECHAPEL;

SOLD BY

DARTON AND HARVEY, GRACECHURCH STREET;

AND

W. EDWARDS, AVE-MARIA LANE, PATERNOSTER ROW.

Price Ninepence sewed, or One Shilling bound.

1837

WISDOM INSTRUCTING YOUTH

THE YOUNG SCHOLARS Manual OF USEFUL KNOWLEDGE,

BY THOS. CARPENTER

Author of the Scholars Spelling Assistant, School Speaker &c &c

LONDON.

Printed and Published by Nath!. Mead, 93. Whitechapel High St.

and by Darton & Harvey, Gracechurch Street and W. Edwards.

Ave Maria Lane. Paternoster Row.

1837.

Price 9d neatly bound or to Purchasers

INTRODUCTION.

THIS little Work is not designed to interfere with other productions of a more comprehensive and descriptive character; but simply to facilitate the improvement of the young scholar in the elementary branches of useful knowledge, without subjecting him to any thing of a prolix or complicated nature, so that the whole may be more easily learned, and better retained. The Author thinks it right to state, that he has gleaned from other sources some little valuable information, which he has endeavoured to embody in a more compendious form, with a view to offer encouragement to the Pupil, and to lessen the toil of the Teacher. Should it meet with the approbation of those for whose use it is principally intended, the Author will derive to himself the most pleasing satisfaction in having contributed his efforts, in however trifling a degree, to smooth the rugged paths which impede the course of a preliminary liberal education.

THE

YOUNG SCHOLAR'S

LITTLE MANUAL.

———◆———

CHAPTER I.

Question. NAME the days of the week.

Answer. Sunday, Monday, Tuesday, Wednesday, Thursday, Friday, and Saturday.

Q. Name the months of the year.

A. January, February, March, April, May, June, July, August, September, October, November, and December.

Q. Repeat the number of days in each month.

A. Thirty days hath September,
April, June, and November,
February has twenty-eight alone,*
And all the rest have thirty-one.

Q. What are the four quarter days?

A. Lady-day,† Midsummer-day,‡ Michaelmas-day,§ and Christmas-day.||

Q. When is the longest day?

Except in leap-year, or every fourth year, when February has ty-nine days.

March 25th.   ‡ June 24th.   § September 29th. || December 5th.

A. The twenty-first of June.

Q. When is the shortest day?

A. The twenty-first of December.

Q. How is the day divided?

A. Into morning, noon, afternoon, and evening.

Q. What are the four chief points of the compass?

A. North, south, east, and west.

Q. What is the circumference of the earth?

A. Three hundred and sixty degrees.

Q. What is a degree?

A. Sixty-nine miles and a half.

Q. How many miles is it round the earth?

A. Twenty-five thousand and twenty.

Q. What is the square of 2?   A. Four.

Q. What is the cube of 2?   A. Eight.

Q. How many sheets make a quire of paper?

A. Twenty-four.

Q. How many trusses make a load of hay?

A. Thirty-six.

Q. What should each truss weigh?

A. Fifty-six pounds.

Q. What is a ton of straw?

A. One load and a half.

Q. What weight is a truss of straw?

A. Thirty-six pounds.

Q. What is a stone of meat?

A. Eight pounds.

Q. What weight is a sack of potatoes?

A. Two hundred.

Q. How many bushels make a sack of flour?

A. Five.

Q. What is a quarter of grain?
A. Eight bushels.
Q. How many sacks of coals make a ton?
A. Ten.
Q. What should each sack weigh?
A. Two hundred and twenty-four pounds.
Q. What is a rod of walling?
A. Two hundred and seventy-two feet and one quarter.
Q. What is a square of flooring?
A. One hundred feet.
Q. What is a stack of wood?
A. One hundred and eight solid feet.
Q. How many feet make a load of hewn timber?   A. Fifty.
Q. What is a *hand* measure?*
A. Four inches.

———

CHAPTER II.

Q. How many principal colours are there?
A. Seven:—red, orange, yellow, green, blue, indigo, and violet.
Q. Name the four elements.
A. Earth, air, fire, and water.
Q. Mention the chief metals.
A. Gold, silver, platina, quicksilver (or mercury,) copper, iron, lead, and tin.
Q. Point out the four cardinal virtues.
A. Prudence, temperance, justice, and fortitude.

* This measure is used to ascertain the height of horses.

A 3

Q. How many senses belong to men and animals?

A. Five:—Hearing, seeing, smelling, tasting and feeling.

Q. What are the different stages of human life?

A. Childhood, youth, manhood, and old age.

Q. What is meant by the Latin words *Anno Domini?*

A. The year of our Lord.

Q. What is signified by the expression *Anno Mundi?*

A. The year of the world.

Q. How tall are most men and women?

A. From five to six feet.

Q. When do persons leave off growing?

A. Between the ages of nineteen and twenty-one.

Q. What is the middle age of man's life?

A. Between forty and fifty.

Q. When does old age begin to show itself?

A. At the age of fifty or sixty years.

Q. Who first discovered the art of printing?

A. Faust, a native of Strasburgh, in Germany.

Q. Who introduced it into England?

A. Caxton, a mercer of London, in 1471.

Q. On what were books formerly written?

A. Barks of trees, tablets of wax, &c.

Q. Who were the inventors of the letters of the alphabet?*   A. The Phœnicians.

---

* These letters were introduced into Europe by Cadmus, king of Thebes, about 1500 years before the birth of Christ.

Q. How many bones are there in the human body?

A. Two hundred and forty-eight.

Q. Of what use are the hairs of the head?

A. To keep open the pores for perspiration.

Q. Are not the hairs hollow? A. Yes.

Q. What is the population of the earth?

A. Eight hundred millions.

Q. What is the population of Europe?

A. About two hundred millions.

Q. How deep is the sea?

A. Perhaps four or five miles, more or less.*

Q. How big is the sun?

A. A million of times larger than the earth.

Q. How far is the sun from the earth?

A. Ninety-five millions of miles.

Q. What is the sun supposed to be?

A. An immense globe of fire.†

Q. What is the diameter of the sun?

A. Eight hundred and eighty-three thousand, two hundred and forty miles.

Q. How far is the moon from the earth?

A. Two hundred and forty thousand miles.

Q. What gives light to the earth, the moon, and the stars?

A. The sun.

Q. What is the moon?

A. A dark body, like our earth.

Q. Is not the moon bigger than the earth?

---

* Dr. Rudge, in his lectures on the Book of Genesis, has a remark that the sea is said to be *eleven* miles deep in some parts; but this is probably over-rated.

† Dr. Herschell gives it as his opinion, that the sun is inhabited.

A. No; it is fifty times less.

Q. What is the moon's diameter?

A. About two thousand one hundred, and seventy-two miles.

Q. In what time does the light come to the earth from the sun?

A. Eight minutes.

Q. How high are the clouds?

A. About half a mile, a mile, or two miles high.

Q. Is air lighter than water?

A. Yes; about eight hundred and sixteen times.

Q. How are tides occasioned?

A. By the attraction of the moon.

Q. What produce earthquakes?

A. The explosion of nitrous and sulphurous vapours pent up in the bowels of the earth.

Q. At what rate does a ray of light travel?

A. At the rate of 193,000 miles an hour.*

Q. What are *cardinal* winds?

A. They are such as blow from the cardinal points of the compass—North, East, South, and West.

Q. What are *collateral* winds?

A. Such as blow between these points.

Q. What are *trade* winds?

A. Such as blow from some given point constantly, or with periodical regularity.

* It moves a million of times faster than a cannon ball.

CHAPTER III.

Q. Of what is bread made?

A. The flour of wheat;* mixed with salt, yeast, and water.

Q. How is butter made?

A. By agitating cream in a churn.

Q. How is cheese made?

A. From milk, by curdling it with rennet.

Q. What is rennet?

A. The stomach or maw of a calf.

Q. How is cheese coloured?

A. With Spanish arnetto.

Q. What is coffee?

A. The berry of a tree.

Q. Where do these trees grow?

A. In Arabia, Turkey, and the West Indies.

Q. Where does sugar come from?

A. The East and West Indies.

Q. What is cocoa?

A. The berry of a tree, which grows in the West Indies.

Q. What is chocolate?

A. A paste made from the cocoa nut.

Q. What is pepper?

A. The produce of a shrub.

Q. Where does this shrub thrive?

A. In the islands of Java and Sumatra.†

Q. What countries produce rice?

---

* Rye or barley is sometimes used in the making of this necessary and nutritious article of life.

† See these on the map of the world.

A. Egypt, the East Indies, and South America.

Q. Where does cinnamon grow?

A. In the islands of Borneo and Ceylon.

Q. What is cochineal?*

A. An insect found in Mexico, &c.

Q. What are nutmegs?

A. The kernel of a large fruit like a walnut.

Q. Where do they grow?

A. In the Molucca isles.

Q. What is mace?

A. A well-known spice.

Q. What are cloves?

A. The blossom buds of the clove tree.

Q. What is sago?

A. The kernel of a fruit of a species of palm.†

Q. What is tapioca?

A. The root of a South American plant called *Cassava.*

Q. From whence have we rhubarb?

A. From Turkey.

Q. What is opium?

A. The juice of the white poppy.‡

Q. What is castor oil?

A. An oil extracted from a nut, the produce of a shrub called *Palmectnester.*

Q. Where does this shrub grow?

A. In Jamaica, and many parts of America.

---

* Pro. kutsh-y-neel.

† Mace, cloves, and sago, are the produce of the Molucca isles.

‡ It is imported from Natolia in Asiatic Turkey, Egypt, and the East Indies.—Laudanum is prepared from it.

Q. What is bark?

A. The outside of a tree which grows chiefly in Peru.

Q. What is ipecacuhana?

A. The root of a shrub which grows in Peru and the Brazils.

Q. What is camphor?

A. A white resinous juice of a kind of bay tree.

Q. Where does it grow?

A. In China, Japan, &c.

Q. What is manna?

A. A gum that oozes from the ash tree in Calabria.

Q. What is tartar?

A. An acrid salt from fermented wines.

Q. Where does liquorice grow?

A. In England; viz. in Yorkshire, Godalming in Surrey, &c.

Q. What is musk?

A. A substance contained in the pouch of an animal, called *Moschus*.

Q. From whence comes musk?

A. Tonquin, China, and Java.

Q. What is myrrh?

A. A sort of gum resin that oozes from a tree which grows in Arabia.

Q. What are galls?

A. Plants brought from Aleppo, in the Levant.*

Q. What is alum?

* Or *eastern* part of the Mediterranean.

A. A fossil salt mineral.

Q. What is saltpetre ?

A. A nitre or salt extracted from earths.

Q. What is sal ammoniac ?

A. A salt obtained from the decomposition of wool, horn, bones, &c.

Q. What is hartshorn ?

A. Water impregnated with sal ammoniac.

Q. What is vitriol ?

A. A fossil salt—a mixture of copper with sulphuric acid.

Q. What is honey ?

A. The produce of bees.

Q. What is hemp ?

A. A plant similiar to flax.

Q. What is tow ?

A. The refuse of hemp.

Q. What is ivory ?

A. The teeth of the elephant.

CHAPTER IV.

Q. WHAT is cork ?

A. The bark of the cork tree.

Q. What countries produce the best ash ?

A. Spain and Portugal.

Q. Where does mahogany come from ?

A. The bay of Honduras, and the West India islands.

Q. What is charcoal ?

A. Wood half burned.

Q. What is spunge ?

A. A marine substance found in the Mediterranean and Indian seas.

Q. What is Indian rubber ?

A. A resin which exudes from two or three species of trees growing in the East Indies.

Q. What is turpentine ?

A. A gum oozing from the pine tree.

Q. What is tar ?

A. A substance obtained by burning foine and fir trees.

Q. How is pitch made ?

A. From tar boiled down to dryness.

Q. How is glue made ?

A. From the skins and sinews of animals, &c.

Q. What is size ?

A. The shreds and parings of leather and parchment boiled in water.

Q. How is rosin made ?

A. By distilling turpentine to dryness.

Q. What is fullers' earth?

A. A marl or earth found in Bedfordshire, and other English counties ?

Q. How is glass made ?

A. With sand, stones or flints, and alkaline salt.

Q. Of what are bricks and tiles made ?

A. Clay, sand, and ashes.

Q. From whence have we slates ?

A. They are dug out of mines in different parts of England.

Q. What is mortar ?

A. A cement made of lime, hair, and water.

Q. Of what are needles made ?

A. Of steel.

Q. Of what are pins made ?

A. Brass drawn out into wire.

Q. Whence comes tobacco ?

A. Chiefly from Virginia, in North America.

Q. What is tobacco ?

A. The leaves of an American plant cut small.

Q. What is snuff ?

A. Tobacco leaves ground into powder.

Q. What is starch ?

A. The sediment of wheat steeped in water.

Q. Of what are candles made ?

A. Tallow.*

Q. What is train oil ?

A. The fat of whales.

Q. What is linseed oil ?

A. Oil made from the seed of flax.

Q. How is sweet oil made ?

A. From olives, which grow in Italy.†

Q. What is gas ?

A. Inflammable air found in coal, &c.

Q. What is isinglass ?

A. The sounds of the cod, ling, &c.

Q. Where is the anchovy found ?

A. In the Mediterranean Sea.

Q. What is vermicelli ?

A. A composition of flour, cheese, yolk of eggs, sugar and saffron.

---

* Russia tallow is the best.

† *Florence* oil is decidedly superior to any other.

Q. What makes ketchup ?
A. Mushrooms.
Q. From what is mustard made ?
A. From the mustard seed.
Q. What makes vinegar ?
A. Wine, beer, or cyder, made sour, and fermented in the sun.
Q. Where do capers come from ?
A. Toulon and Lyons in the south of France.
Q. What is ivory black ?
A. The shavings of ivory burnt in a crucible to a black powder.
Q. How are wafers made ?
A. With a mixture of flour, white of eggs, isinglass, and a little yeast.
Q. What makes paper ?
A. Linen rags, &c. beaten to a pulp in water.
Q. What is parchment ?
A. The skins of sheep or goats.
Q. How is black ink made ?
A. With galls, green vitriol, gum arabic, and water.
Q. How is red ink made ?
A. With Brazil wood, gum arabic, alum, and white sugar, infused in vinegar.
Q. How is Indian ink made ?
A. With lamp black and animal glue.
Q. What makes gunpowder ?
A. Saltpetre, sulphur, and charcoal.
Q. What is verdigrease ?
A. A copperas substance.
Q. What is shagreen ?
A. The skin of the shark.

CHAPTER V.

Q. WHAT is the atmosphere ?

A. The body of air which surrounds the earth.

Q. What is twilight ?

A. The day-light after the sun sets.*

Q. What has the air to do with sound ?

A. It receives and conveys sounds to the ear.

Q. How are sounds produced ?

A. By the motion of bodies in the air.

Q. What is an eclipse of the sun ?

A. The moon passing between the earth and the sun.

Q. What is an eclipse of the moon ?

A. The earth passing between the sun and moon.

Q. What is lightning ?

A. The discharge of electrical fire in the clouds.

Q. What is thunder ?

A. The bursting of clouds which lightning occasions.

Q. What is wind ?

A. Streams of air put in motion by heat, cold, or some other cause.

Q. What is rain ?

A. Moist vapours, which fall down in the form of drops of water.†

---

* It remains *two hours* after the sun sets, and which appears again before he rises.

† That is, when they become too heavy to be supported by the atmosphere.

Q. What are clouds ?

A. Watery vapours collected and suspended in the atmosphere.

Q. What is fog or mist ?

A. Vapours rising and hovering near the surface of the earth.

Q. How is the rainbow produced ?

A. By the rays of the sun on the falling drops of rain.

Q. What is snow ?

A. The watery particles of fogs, &c. congealed by cold.

Q. What is hail ?

A. Frozen drops of rain.

Q. What is the milky way ?

A. A vast assemblage of fixed stars, too distant for the naked eye.

CHAPTER VI.

Q. How are the Holy Scriptures divided ?

A. Into two books.

Q. What are these two books called ?

A. The Old Testament and the New Testament.*

Q. How many books are contained in the Old Testament ?

A. Forty-nine.

Q. Who wrote the first five books ?

* Both together, form what is called the BIBLE.

A 9

A. Moses.

Q. What are they called ?

A. The Pentateuch.

Q. Name the prophetical books.

A. Isaiah, Jeremiah, Ezekiel, and Daniel.

Q. In what language was the Old Testament originally written ?

A. The Hebrew.*

Q. Into how many books is the New Testament divided ?

A. Twenty-seven.

Q. Particularize them.

A. The four Gospels, the Acts of the Apostles, the Epistles, and the Book of Revelation.

Q. In what language was the New Testament first written ?

A. The Greek.

Q. When was the Bible first translated into English ?

A. In the year 1534.†

Q. By whom ?

A. Tindal and Coverdale.

Q. Who was the founder of the Christian religion ?

A. Jesus Christ, the Son of God.

Q. How long was it, after the creation of the world, that he appeared on the earth ?

A. Four thousand years.

---

* Supposed to have been formed by God himself, and supernaturally communicated to the first man, *Adam ;* consequently it is the oldest or primitive language, and has been called the most *emphatical* in the world.

† In four years afterwards it was read in the English churches.

Q. How long was our Saviour engaged in his divine ministry?

A. Twenty-one years.*

Q. Was not God in Christ?   A. Yes.

Q. What does the word *Jesus* signify?

A. A Saviour

Q. What is meant by Christ's incarnation?

A. That he took our nature upon him, and became man.

Q. What is meant by his nativity?

A. The day when he was born.

Q. What by his passion?

A. His death and sufferings on the cross.

Q. What by his atonement?

A. His " propitiation," or dying " for the sins of the whole world."

CHAPTER VII.

Q. WHAT is arithmetic?

A. The art of computation.

Q. What is architecture?

A. The art of building.

Q. How many orders of architecture are there?

A. Five.

Q. Name them.

A. The Tuscan, the Doric, the Ionic, the Corinthian, and the Composite.

* From his twelfth year to the time of his ascension into heaven.

Q. What is agriculture ?

A. The art of tilling or cultivating the ground

Q. What is astronomy ?

A. The knowledge of the heavenly bodies; the sun, moon, planets, stars, comets, &c.

Q. What is biogragphy ?

A. The history of learned and scientific men.

Q. What is botany ?

A. That knowledge which shows the kinds, forms, virtues, and uses of plants, flowers, and vegetables.

Q. What is chronology ?

A. The relation which describes particular events, &c.

Q. What is electricity ?

A. Attraction produced by means of conductors chemically.

Q. What is engraving ?

A. The art of excavating metals, seals, marble, &c., so as to represent on them figures, letters, &c.

Q. Mention the fine arts.

A. Poetry, music, painting, sculpture, and engraving.

Q. What is geography ?

A. A description of the earth, as consisting of land and water.

Q. What is history ?

A. A narration of historical events.

Q. What is mineralogy ?

A. The science of natural history.

Q. What is mythology ?

A. The history and description of the fabulous deities of the heathen world.

Q. What is music?

A. A succession of sounds which excite agreeable sensations.

Q. What is meteorology?

A. The science which teaches the phenomena of the atmosphere.

Q. What is meant by optics?

A. The science of vision.

Q. What is pharmacy?

A. The art of preserving and intermixing medicines.

Q. What is implied by statics?

A. The art of weighing bodies.

Q. What is typography?

A. The art of printing.

Q. What is autography?

A. An original writing.

Q. What is to be understood by heraldry?

A. The art of blazoning and marshalling coats of arms.

Q. What is philosophy?

A. The love and pursuit of knowledge and wisdom.

Q. Into how many branches is philosophy divided?

A. Into four; namely, metaphysical, intellectual, physical, and moral.

Q. What is zoölogy?

A. The branch of natural history which relates to animals.

Questions and Answers

IN

ENGLISH GRAMMAR.

—•—

CHAPTER I.

Q. WHAT does English Grammar teach?

A. The art of speaking and writing the English language in a correct and proper manner.

Q. How many letters are there in the English alphabet?

A. Twenty-six; viz. *a, b, c, d, e, f, g, h, i, j, k, l, m, n, o, p, q, r, s, t, u, v, w, x, y, z.*

Q. How are the letters divided?

A. Into vowels and consonants.

Q. What number of vowels are there?

A. Five; viz. *a, e, i, o,* and *u.*

Q. When are *w* and *y* vowels?

A. When they *end* a word or syllable?

Q. Can you make a syllable or word without a vowel?

A. No.

Q. What is a monosyllable?

A. A word of one syllable; as, *cat, dog.*

Q. What is a dissyllable?

A. A word of two syllables; as, *master, content.*

Q. What is a trisyllable ?

A. A word of three syllables ; as, *improper*, *consider*.

Q. What is a polysyllable ?

A. A word of four or more syllables; as, *improperly*, *unnecessary*.

Q. What is a *proper* name or word ?

A. A name given to men, kingdoms, cities, rivers, and mountains ; as, *Thomas, England, London, Thames, Mount Vesuvius.*

Q. What is a *common* name or word ?

A. *All* substantives which are not *proper* names are *common* ; as, *bread, boy, man, tea, sugar,* &c.

Q. What is a *primitive* word ?

A. A word which cannot be altered to any simpler word; as, *hot, pen, sober.*

Q. What is a *derivative* word ?

A. A word which may or can be reduced to another word ; as, *hotter, penny, soberly.*

Q. How many parts of speech are there ?

A. Nine.

Q. Name them ?

A. The article, the substantive or noun, the adjective, the pronoun, the verb, the adverb, the preposition, the conjunction, and the interjection.

———

CHAPTER II.

Q. WHAT is an article ?

A. A word used before substantives, and

other parts of speech, to point them out more clearly; as, *a* school, *an* inkstand, *the* master; *a* useful tool, *the* very best of them, &c.

Q. What is a substantive or noun ?

A. The name of any person, place or thing; as, *William, Whitechapel, book.*

Q. What is an adjective ?

A. The name of a quality; as, a *good* girl, a *bad* pen, a *black* thing.

Q. What is a pronoun ?

A. A word used instead of a noun, so that the same word may not be repeated too frequently; as, the boy is diligent; *he* is obedient; *he* has an amiable temper.

Q. What is a verb ?

A. The name of an action, or the doing of a thing ; as I *dance*, you *write*, she *sings* ; or to *dance*, to *write*, to *sing*.

Q. What is an adverb ?

A. A part of speech added to a verb, an adjective, and sometimes to another adverb, to express some circumstance respecting it; as, he writes *well*, a *truly* dutiful son ; he speaks French *very fluently*.

Q. What are prepositions ?

A. Small words chiefly of *one* syllable, which serve to connect the words with each other; as, he went *from* England *to* France; you may sit *by* him; it was given to him *for* his supper.

Q. What is a conjunction ?

A. A part of speech that is used to connect both words and sentences; as, two *and* two make four; you are healthy, *because* you are temperate.

Q. What are interjections ?

A. Exclamations of joy, grief, and wonder; as, *oh! ah! alas! hush! behold!* &c.

Q. How many articles are there ?

A. Two ; *a* or *an*, and *the*.

Q. When is the article *a* changed into *an?*

A. Before a vowel, and a silent *h ;* as, *an* arm, *an* honest man.

Q. How many numbers are there ?

A. Two.

Q. What are they called?

A. The singular and the plural.

Q. Of what does the singular speak ?

A. But one object; as, a bird, a cage.

Q. What the plural ?

A. More objects than one ; as, birds, cages.

Q. How is the singular number made plural?

A. By adding the letter *s* to the singular ; as, hat, hats ; pen, pens ; top, tops.

Q. Suppose the words end in *ch, sh, ss,* or *x,* how do you form the plural number ?

A. By adding *es* in the plural; as, march, marches; dish, dishes; miss, misses; fox, foxes.

Q. If a word end in *y* in the singular number and a consonant go before it, how would you express the plural ?

A. By changing the *y* into *ies ;* as, lady, ladies; cherry, cherries.

Q. If a vowel precede the *y,* how then ?

A. By adding *s* only ; as, key, keys; pray, prays.

Q. How many degrees of comparison are there ?

A. Three; the positive, the comparative and the superlative.

Q. What is the positive?

A. The adjective in its natural state; as, wise, good, learned.

Q. What is the comparative?

A. The adjective is in the comparative degree when *er* is added to the end of it, or the word *more* is put before it; as, he is wis*er*, or he is *more* learned than you.

Q. What is the superlative degree?

A. It increases or lessens the positive to the highest or lowest degree, and becomes superlative by adding *st* or *est*, to the end of it, or the adverb *most* before it; as, he is the wisest, or the *most* learned of any.*

Q. How many genders are there?

A. Three: the masculine, the feminine, and the neuter gender.

CHAPTER III.

Q. WHAT is meant by the masculine gender?

A. Animals of the male or *he* kind; as, *stag, horse, bull.*

Q. What by the feminine gender?

A. Animals of the female or *she* kind; as, *deer, mare, cow.*

Q. What by the neuter gender?

* Dissyllables and trisyllables are generally compared by the adverbs *more* and *most*; as, tender, *more* tender, *most* tender; delightful, *more* delightful, *most* delightful.

A. Things of neither sex; as, *hat, shoe, house*.

Q. How many cases are there ?

A. Three; the nominative, the genitive, and the accusative.*

Q. What is the nominative case ?

A. The being or thing that acts, and comes before the verb ; as, Martha loves needlework.

Q. What is the genitive case ?

A. It signifies property or possession; as, my father's house.

Q. What is the accusative case ?

A. That which follows a verb active or a preposition; as, I dislike him, he is fond of you.

Q. How is the genitive case formed ?

A. By an apostrophe, (') with the letter *s* coming after it; as, the woman's bonnet.†

Q. Is the apostrophe *s* added when the genitive plural ends in *s* ?

A. No; as, the butchers' stalls ; the Jews' hospital.

Q. Which are the personal pronouns ?

A. *I, thou, he, she, we, ye* or *you*, and *they*.

Q. Which are the possessive pronouns ?

A. *My, thy, his, her, our, your*, and *their*.

Q. What are relative pronouns ?

A. Relative pronouns relate to some word going before ; as, the boy is good *who* minds his business.

Q. What are interrogative pronouns ?

---

* *Possessive* and *objective*, like *substantive* and *noun*, are synonymous terms, or expressions of the same meaning.

† The apostrophe *s* when several names occur together, is added to the *last* only ; as, Richard, Henry, and Frederick's garden.

A. Those which are used in asking questions; as, *who* are you ? *which* is the book ? *what* are you about ?

Q. How many sorts of pronouns are there ?

A. Three; the personal, the relative, and adjective pronouns.

Q. How many sorts of verbs are there ?

A. Three; the active, the neuter, and the passive.

Q. What are participles ?

A. They are parts of speech derived from a verb; as *loving, loved, having loved.*

Q. What are moods ?

A. The different methods of expressing our intentions.

Q. How many moods are there ?

A. Five ; the *indicative*, the *imperative*, the *potential*, the *subjunctive*, and the *infinitive.*

Q. What is meant by the word tense ?

A. The distinction of time.

Q. Mention the six variations.

A. The *present*, the *imperfect*, the *perfect*, the *pluperfect*, and the *first* and *second future.*

Q. What do you mean by the conjugation of a verb ?

A. To conjugate a verb is to show the different variations or changes that it undergoes, in *number, person, mood* and *tense.**

Q. What is parsing ?

A. To resolve the parts of speech by grammar rules.

---

* Here let the young scholar refer to his grammar, and repeat what is necessary to be learned or understood.

Q. What is punctuation?

A. The art of using certain points or stops, so as to mark the sense in writing, and to read with greater propriety.

Q. Point out the several points and stops?

A. A *comma* , a *semicolon* ; a *colon* : a *period* or *full stop* . a *note of interrogation?* a *note of admiration !*

Q. What is syntax?

A. A part of grammar which treats of the agreement and construction of words in a sentence.*

Questions and Answers

ON THE

MAP OF THE WORLD.

CHAPTER I.

Q. Name the four quarters of the world?

A. Europe, Asia, Africa, and America.†

---

* As this little performance, so limited in extent, is not intended to supersede existing publications on English Grammar, the teacher will not of course expect to find a full amplification in so important and useful a study, but merely regard it as an attempt at once simple and introductory.

† The term *Australia* has been adopted by modern geographers to denote the numerous islands in the great Pacific Ocean, which by some are classed under two names, viz. *Australasia* and *Polynesia.*

Q. What does the eastern continent (or *hemisphere*) comprehend?

A. Europe, Asia, and Africa.

Q. What does the western continent comprehend?

A. North and South America.

Q. How are North and South America joined together?

A. By the isthmus of Darien, or Panamá.

Q. What is an isthmus?

A. A narrow part of land by which a peninsula is joined to a continent or main land.

Q. Which is the largest island in the world?

A. New Holland.

Q. Where is Van Dieman's land?

A. To the south-east of New Holland.

Q. Name the five great oceans?

A. The Atlantic, the Pacific, the Indian, the Northern, and the Southern Oceans.

Q. Where is the Indian Ocean?

A. To the south of Asia.*

Q. Is there more water than land?

A. Yes: the land is about one-fourth, and the water three-fourths of the whole surface.

Q. What islands lie between North and South America?

A. The West India islands.

Q. What two large capes stretch out into the Southern Ocean?

A. The Cape of Good Hope, and Cape Horn.†

* It extends from Africa on the west to New Holland on the east.

† Cape Horn stretches the farther south.

Q. Name the island at the foot of Hindostan.

A. Ceylon.

Q. How is Africa joined to Asia ?

A. By the isthmus of Suez.

Q. What ocean divides Europe and Africa from North and South America ?

A. The Atlantic Ocean.*

Q. What ocean separates America from Asia.

A. The Pacific Ocean.†

Q. Where is the Red Sea ?

A. Between Arabia and Egypt.

Q. Where are the Brazils ?

A. In South America.

Q. Where are Behring's Straits ?

A. Between the north-east of Asia, and the north-west of America.

Q. Where is Iceland ?

A. In the Northern Ocean near Greenland.

CHAPTER II.

Q. WHAT sea divides Europe from Africa ?

A. The Mediterranean Sea.

---

* It takes its name from *Mount Atlas* in the north-west of Africa.

† The word *Pacific* derives its name from the winds of that ocean blowing uniformly from east to west; so that ships in sailing from the west coast of America to Asia, never require to shift their sails during the voyage.

Q. What straits lead from the Atlantic Ocean into the Mediterranean Sea ?

A. The straits of Gibraltar.

Q. What sea lies between Sweden and Russia ?

A. The Baltic Sea.

Q. Where is the island of Terra-del-Fuego ?

A. It is situated on the southern extremity of America.

Q. What straits separate Van Dieman's land from New Holland ?

A. Bass Straits.

Q. Where is the Gulf of Florida ?

A. South-east of Florida in North America.

Q. Where is Baffin's Bay ?

A. North of Davis' Straits.

Q. Which do you call the Caribbean Sea ?

A. Where the Caribbee West India Islands are.*

Q. Where is Greenland ?

A. Greenland is a large country of the arctic seas, celebrated for its whale fishery.

Q. Are there many islands in the Pacific Ocean ?

A. Yes; and in one of which, (*O-why-hee,*) Captain Cook was killed in 1779.

Q. Of what part of the world is Newfoundland ?

A. It lies on the eastern coast of North America, viz. east of the Gulf of St. Lawrence.

Q. Which is the largest river in the world ?

* So called from *Caraib*, the ancient inhabitants.

A. The Amazon, or more properly *Maranon*, of South America.

Q. Name the largest lake in the world?

A. Lake Superior, in North America.*

Q. Where are the islands of Bombay and Ceylon?

A. Bombay lies west of Hindostan in Asia; and Ceylon is situated at the foot of Hindostan.

Q. Where are the Bahama or Lucca Islands?

A. They lie south-east of Florida.

Q. Where are Davis's Straits?

A. On the coast of Greenland, leading to Baffin's Bay.

Q. How are the Falkland isles situated?

A. On the east of Patagonia in South America.

Q. How far is the equator from the North and South Poles?

A. One hundred and eighty degress.

Q. Which is the largest quarter of the world?

A. America.

Q. Which is the smallest quarter of the world? A. Europe.

Q. Name the great circles of the globe?

A. The meridian, the equator, the horizon, the ecliptic, and the two colures.

Q. Point out the small circles.

A. The tropic of Cancer, the tropic of Capricorn, the polar circles, the Arctic, and Antarctic.

---

* Lake Superior is more than 400 miles long, and has on it many islands. The passage between the lakes Ontario and Erie is interrupted by a stupendous cataract (or fall of water) called the falls of Niagara, 150 feet in height, in the form of a half moon. The noise of this fall is heard at the distance of 15 miles.

Questions and Answers

ON THE

MAP OF EUROPE.

CHAPTER I.

Q. How is Europe bounded?

A. On the north by the Frozen Ocean; south by the Mediterranean Sea; east by Asia; and west by the Atlantic Ocean.

Q. Name the chief countries of Europe.

A. Sweden (including Norway), Russia, Denmark, Prussia, Germany, Turkey, France, Holland, Belgium, Switzerland, Italy, Spain, Portugal, and the United Kingdom of Great Britain and Ireland.

Q. Which is the largest island in Europe?

A. Great Britain.

Q. What sea washes the eastern coast of England?

A. The North Sea.

Q. What channel flows between England and France?

A. The English Channel.

Q. What channel lies between England and Ireland?

A. St. George's Channel.

Q. Where are the two peninsulas called the Morea and the Crimea?

A. The Morea is in Greece, and the Crimea in the Black Sea.

Q. What straits lead from the Archipelago to the Black Sea ?

A. The straits of Constantinople.

Q. Where is the Bay of Biscay ?

A. Between France and Spain.

Q. Name the islands in the Mediterranean Sea.

A. Ivica, Majorca, Minorca, Elba, Sicily, Malta, Candia, Cyprus, &c.

Q. How is Europe separated from America ?

A. By the Atlantic Ocean.

Q. How is Africa separated from Asia?

A. By the Pacific Ocean.

Q. Name the Iönian isles ?

A. Corfu, Faxo, Santa-Maura, Cephalonia, Ithaca, Zante, and Cerigo.*

Q. Where are the straits of Messina ?

A. Between Italy and Sicily.

Q. How are the Uralian mountains situated ?

A. To the north-east of Russia.

Q. What kingdom lies next to Holland on the sea side ?

A. France.

Q. What mountains divide France from Spain ?

A. The Pyrenees.

Q. Name the sea between Italy and Turkey.

* These seven islands are at the entrance of the Gulf of Venice, or the Adriatic Sea; the six first stand west of Greece, and the last, south of the peninsula, called the *Morea* ; they form a free state, under the protection of the King of Great Britain, in whom the executive is invested.

A. The Adriatic Sea, or Gulf of Venice.

Q. Are there any volcanoes in Europe?

A. Yes; there are three: Mount Vesuvius, in Italy; Mouut Etna, in Sicily; and Mount Hecla, in the cold island of Iceland.

Q. What is the Archipelago?

A. A cluster of many islands, contiguous to the Mediterranean Sea.

Q. What is the general summary of

EUROPE ?

Nations.	Chief Cities.	Inhabitants.	Miles from London.
Sweden	Stockholm	3 millions	895
Russia*	Petersburgh	36 millions	1265
Poland	Warsaw	13½ millions	640
Denmark	Copenhagen	3 millions	565
Prussia	Berlin	10 millions	599
Netherlands	Amsterdam	6 millions	206
German States†	Dresden	25 millions	590
Austria	Vienna	28 millions	780
Turkey‡	Constantinople	8 millions	1500
France	Paris	29 millions	210
Switzerland	Berne	2 millions	445
Italy and Naples	Rome	10 millions	863
Portugal	Lisbon	4 millions	1010
Spain	Madrid	11 millions	802
Great Britain and Ireland§	London	16 millions	

* Russia has 5,000,000 in Asia.

† Including the population of Hanover, Wirtemburg, Saxony, and Bavaria.

‡ Turkey has 10,000,000 in Asia, and 2,500,000 in Egypt, making in the whole 18,500,000.

§ The ancient name of England was *Britannia,* so called by the *Romans;* of Ireland, *Hibernia,* so called by *Cæsar, Tacitus,* and *Pliny;* and of Scotland, *Caledonia,* so called by *Tacitus.* Pliny says the ancient name of England was *Albion;* but that *Britannia,* a name of the same meaning, became the prevalent appellation.

𝕼𝖚𝖊𝖘𝖙𝖎𝖔𝖓𝖘 𝖆𝖓𝖉 𝕬𝖓𝖘𝖜𝖊𝖗𝖘

ON THE

MAP OF ASIA.

—◆—

CHAPTER I.

Q. How is Asia bounded?

A. On the north, by the Northern or Arctic Ocean; south, by the Indian Ocean; west, by Europe, the Black Sea, Archipelago, Levant, and Red Sea; and east, by the Pacific Ocean.

Q. Mention the chief countries in Asia.

A. Russia, Tartary, Siberia, &c., Circassia and Georgia, (annexed to Russia,) Independent Tartary, Tibet, Arabia, and several others in the Turkish Empire, Persia, Cabul, Hindostan, British India, Birman Empire, Cochin-China and Tonquin, Chinese Empire, and Japanese Empire.

Q. Which is the largest of the Asiatic isles?

A. Borneo, north of Java.

Q. Point out (on the map) Tonquin, Canton, Astracan, Mecca, Medina, Pekin, Bombay, Madras, and Calcutta.

A. [Here the pupil will do as desired.]

Q. Where is the city of Ispahan?

A. In the Persian Empire.

Q. How is the island of Madagascar situated?

B

A. It lies in the Indian Ocean, east of Africa.

Q. Where are the straits of Babelmandel?

A. Between the Indian Ocean and the Red Sea.

Q. Where are the Philippine isles?

A. In the China Sea.

Q. What ocean lies on the south of Asia?

A. The Indian Ocean.

Q. Where is Swan River?

A. On the west of New Holland.

Q. What two large islands does the equator pass through?

A. Borneo and Sumatra.

Q. Where is the sea of Kamtschatka?

A. East of Siberia.

Q. Point out the Gulf of Persia on the map.

A. See the map of Asia.

Q. Where is Cairo?

A. In Egypt, on the east side of the Nile.

Q. Where is the Whang-hay, or Yellow Sea?

A. North-east of China.

Q. What is the general summary of

ASIA?

Nations.	Chief Cities.	Inhabitants.	Miles from London.
Turkey	Aleppo	10 millions	2980
Russia	Astracan	5 millions	2149
China	Pekin	150 millions	4999
Tonquin	Bachin	21 millions	
Japan	Jeddo	30 millions	5942
Birman Empire	Ava	17 millions	5346
Siam	Siam	8 millions	5560
Hindostan	Calcutta	85 millions	4928
Persia	Ispahan	10 millions	2951
Tartary	Samarcand	10 millions	3127
Arabia	Mecca	10 millions	2988

Questions and Answers

ON THE

MAP OF AFRICA.

——◆——

CHAPTER I.

Q. How is Africa bounded?

A. North by the Mediterranean Sea; south by the Southern Ocean; west by the Atlantic Ocean; east by the Indian Ocean, the Red Sea, and the isthmus of Suez, which unites it to Asia.

Q. Where are St. Helena, Table Bay, and Madeira?

A. St. Helena * is in the Ethiopian Ocean; Table Bay, north-west of the Cape of Good Hope; and Madeira in the Atlantic Ocean, opposite Barbary, in Africa.

Q. What are the principal islands belonging to Africa?

A. The Canaries, Madagascar, Mauritius or Isle of France, Bourbon, St. Helena, Madeira, Cape de Verd Isles, and the Azores.†

Q. Point out Sierra Leone.

---

* This small but important island is possessed by the English. It contains about three thousand inhabitants, and is remarkable for the exile and death of Buonaparte, one of the most extraordinary characters of modern times.

† Let the pupil accurately trace these islands on the map.

A. It stands on the west coast in Upper Guinea, and is a British Settlement,* but extremely unhealthy, and fatal to the lives of Europeans.

Q. What is the name of the river that flows through Abyssinia, Nubia, and Egypt?

A. The Nile, the source of which is doubtful.

Q. Where is Algiers?

A. East of Fez, in Africa.†

Q. Where the mountains of the moon?

A. South-east of Negroland.

Q. Is Cairo situated near the Nile?

A. Yes; it stands on the east side of it.‡

Q. Where is Alexandria?

A. North-west on the coast of Egypt, built by Alexander the Great.

Q. Where does Zaara, or the Great Desert lie?

A. South of the Barbary States.§

Q. Point out Rosetta and Damiette on the map.

A. See the map.

Q. Into what sea does the river Nile empty itself?

A. The Mediterranean Sea.

Q. Is there any other great river in Africa?

* Etablished in the year 1791.

† *Constantia*, which resisted the late French attack or invasion is seventy-five miles inland, south-west from Bona.

‡ Nearly opposite to Cairo, west of the Nile, are the Pyramids, those mighty masses. There are seven, of which the largest is 700 feet square at the base, and above 500 feet in height, and covers eleven acres of ground.

§ This desert extends from the Atlantic coast to Egypt and Nubia, comprehending a space of about two thousand miles from east to west, and one hundred in breadth.

A. Yes, the Niger; and there are also the Senegal, Gambia, and Congo rivers, which last, by a circuitous course, flows south-west into the Atlantic Ocean.

Q. What channel flows between Africa and Madagascar?

A. The Mosambique Channel.

Q. Point out the rivers, the seas, the gulfs, and principal places in this quarter of the world.

A. Consult the map.

Q. Where is the Gulf of Guinea?

A. South of Upper Guinea.

Q. Where is Cape Verd?

A. West of Negroland.

Q. Is not Teneriffe one of the Canary isles?

A. Yes.

Q. For what is it celebrated?

A. For the mountain called the *Peak*, which is the loftiest single mountain in the world, being three miles in height.

Q. What is the general summary of

AFRICA ?*

Nations.	Chief Cities.	Inhabitants.	Miles from London.
Abyssinia	Gondar	2 millions	3376
Egypt	Cairo	2½ millions	2183
Morocco, Fez,&c.	Morocco	15 millions	1459
Algiers	Algiers	¼ million	1107
Tunis	Tunis	¼ million	1141
Tripoli	Tripoli	½ million	1450

* The continent of *Africa* is one vast peninsula, situated to the south of Europe and to the south-west of Asia. It extends about 5000 miles from north to south, and about 4600 miles in its broadest part, from east to west. The southern part of Africa forms a great promontory, terminated by the *Cape of Good Hope.*

Questions and Answers

ON THE

MAP OF AMERICA.

———

CHAPTER I.

Q. How is America divided?

A. Into North and South America.

Q. Where does America lie?

A. Between the Pacific and Atlantic Ocean.

Q. How is North America bounded?

A. North by the Northern or Arctic Ocean; south by the Gulf of Mexico, Isthmus of Darien, and the Pacific; east by the Atlantic; and west by the Pacific Ocean.

Q. Where is Upper Canada?

A. On the north and east of the great lakes.

Q. Where is Lower Canada?

A. On the north of the United States.

Q. What large lakes are in North America?

A. Lakes Superior, Huron, Erie, and Ontario, between the United States and Upper Canada, and several others.

Q. Where is Quebec?

A. It lies south on the river St. Lawrence.*

---

* Quebec is the capital of British America, and is a well-fortified town. It was taken by the British from the French in 1759, after a gallant victory, in which the brave *General Wolfe* was slain. The extent of the British possessions is about two millions of square miles; and their population between two and three millions.

Q. Point out Baffin's Bay.

A. See the map, and say how it is situated.

Q. What is California?

A. It is a peninsula in the Pacific Ocean, north-west of Mexico.

Q. Is there not a gulf of that name?

A. Yes; it borders on that peninsula.

Q. Point out the island of Cape Breton.

A. East of Nova Scotia.

Q. Where is Hudson's Bay?

A. North of the British possessions.

Q. Where is the Bay of Campeachy?

A. South-west of the Gulf of Mexico.

Q. Is Cape Farewell near Davis' Straits?

A. Yes; and it forms a point between East Greenland and West Greenland.

Q. Where is Nootka Sound?

A. On the west coast near the mouth of the Columbia.

Q. Where is the Gulf of Mexico?

A. South of the United States, and east of Mexico.

Q. What large island lies at the foot of Florida? A. Cuba.

Q. In what ocean are the Bermudas, or Summer Isles?

A. In the Atlantic Ocean, east of the United States.

Q. Into what gulf does the Mississippi empty itself?

A. It flows from Red Lake, west of Lake Superior, south through the United States, and empties itself into the Gulf of Mexico.

CHAPTER II.

Q. How is South America bounded ?

A. North by the Caribbean Sea ; south by the Southern Ocean; east by the Atlantic Ocean ; west by the Pacific Ocean ; and united to North America by the isthmus of Darien.

Q. What cape lies at the extremity of South America ?

A. Cape Horn.

Q. Where is Buenos Ayres and La Plata ?

A. East on the right bank of La Plata, fifty miles from the ocean.

Q. Where is Juan Fernandez ?

A. West of Valparaiso, in Chili.*

Q. What is the name of the capital of Brazil?

A. St. Sebastian, or Rio Janeiro.

Q. Where is Cayonne ?

A. North-east of Surinam, Guiana.†

Q. Point out Bahia or St. Salvader, Mount Video, Chili, St. Jago, Peru, Valparaiso, Trinidad, and the islands of Juan Fernandez, Tobago. Grenada, Jamaica, Cuba, and St. Kits.

A. Refer to the map.

Q. What isles lie south-east of Pantagonia?

A. Falkland Isles.‡

* This island is noted for the adventures of Alexander Selkirk, who lived there alone for some years, and gave rise to the celebrated novel of *Robinson Crusoe.*

† Celebrated for the pungent pepper imported into Europe from that Colony, *(French.) Demerara* is situated north-west, at the mouth of a river of that name.

‡ An uninhabited group.

Q. What island lies near New York?

A. Long Island.

Q. On what river is Quebec?

A. On the St. Lawrence.

Q. Is lake Michigan in North America?

A. Yes; south of Lake Superior.

Q. Which are the four largest lakes in North America?

A. Superior, Huron, Erie, and Ontario, which are the largest in the world.

Q. Name the chief islands in the Caribbean Sea.

A. The principal of the *Leeward* Islands are Antigua, Guadaloupe, and Dominica; and those of the *Windward* range are Martinique, St. Lucie, Grenada, Tobago, Trinidad,* and Barbadoes.

Q. Where are the mouths of the Oronoco river?

A. After this river quits Lake Parima, it flows by a circuitous course through Columbia into the Atlantic.†

Q. How is Vera Cruz situated?

A. East of Mexico, on the Gulf of Mexico.

Q. Into what ocean does the river Amazon empty itself?

A. Into the Atlantic Ocean, at the equator.‡

Q. Where are the straits of Magellan?

A. Between the south of Pantagonia and Terra del Fuego.

* Near the coast of *Columbia*.

† The source of the Oronoco is not yet precisely ascertained.

‡ It rises in the Andes, like all the rivers in South America, near Titicaca, and flows north-east through Brazil.

Q. What is the general summary of

AMERICA ?

Nations.	Chief Cities.	Inhabitants.	Miles from London.
United States	Washington	10 millions	3658
Columbia, Peru, La Plata, &c.	Lima	13 millions	5699
British Dominions	Quebec	2 millions	3161
Empire of Brazil	Rio Janeiro	4 millions	2573

Questions and Answers

ON THE

MAP OF THE BRITISH ISLES.

CHAPTER I.

Q. How is England bounded ?

A. On the north by Scotland ; south by the English Channel ; east by the North Sea ; and west by St. George's Channel and the Irish Sea.

Q. How many counties are there in England?

A. Forty.

Q. Point out the *maritime* counties.*

A. Trace them on the map, and mention the chief towns, rivers, &c.

Q. Where is the Isle of Wight ?

* That is, those bordering on the *sea*.

A. On the Southern Coast, opposite Portsmouth.

Q. What channel flows between England and France?

A. The English Channel.

Q. Where are Jersey, Guernsey, Alderney, and Sark?

A. Near the coast of France.

Q. Name the island off Caernarvonshire.

A. The Isle of Anglesea.

Q. In what sea is the Isle of Man?

A. The Irish Sea.

Q. Point out the Eddystone light-house?

A. Look for the English Channel.

Q. What group of islands lie at the Land's End?

A. Scilly Islands,* south-west of Cornwall.

Q. In what county is Gravesend?

A. Kent.

Q. In what county is London?

A. Middlesex.

Q. Which are called *Cinque Ports?*

A. Dover, Sandwich, Hythe, Romney, south-east of Kent, and Hastings, east of Essex.

Q. Where does the river Thames rise?

A. On the borders of Gloucestershire and Wiltshire, in the Cotswold Hills.†

Q. Into what sea does it empty itself?

A. The North Sea.

---

* Above a hundred in number.

† This noble river divides Oxfordshire from Buckinghamshire and Berkshire; Middlesex from Surrey; and Essex from Kent.

Q. Name the chief cities of England, Scotland, and Ireland.

A. London, Edinburgh, and Dublin.

Q. Which is the smallest division of the island of Great Britain?

A. Wales.

Q. How is Wales situated?

A. It lies on the west of England.

Q. Do all the counties in England touch the sea?　A. No.

Q. What channel lies south of Wales?

A. The Bristol Channel.

Q. What channel lies to the west of Wales?

A. St. George's Channel.

CHAPTER II.

Q. WHAT were the ancient names of England, Ireland, and Scotland?

A. Of England, *Britannia*; Ireland, *Hibernia*; Scotland, *Caledonia*.

Q. How many counties does Wales and Scotland contain?

A. Wales contains twelve counties, and Scotland thirty-three.

Q. What islands lie on the north and west of Scotland?

A. The Shetland Islands, the Orkney Islands, the Hebrides, or Western Islands, &c.

Q. Where are the Cheviot hills?

A. Between England and Scotland.

Q. Point out Glasgow, Dundee, Aberdeen, and St. Andrew's.

A. See the map of Scotland.

Q. How is Ireland separated from England, and how bounded?

A. By the Irish Sea or St. George's Channel, and is bounded on the north, west, and south, by the Atlantic Ocean.

Q. Is Ireland as large as England?

A. No.

Q. Into how many provinces is Ireland divided?

A. Four; viz. *Ulster, Leinster, Munster,* and *Connaught.*

Q. On what river is Dublin situated?

A. The Liffey, which falls into Dublin harbour.

Q. Where is Cape Clear?

A. South of Ireland.

Q. What great ocean lies to the west of Ireland?

A. The Atlantic Ocean.

Q. Where is the Shannon river?

A. It separates the province of Connaught from Leinster and Munster.

Q. Point out the Boyne and other rivers; also the different capes, bays, and islands.

A. See the map of Ireland.

Q. Are there any lakes or loughs in Ireland?

A. Several; as Lough Neagh, Lough Erne, Lough Allen, &c.

Q. How many counties are there in Ireland?

A. Thirty-two.

Promiscuous Questions

IN

GEOGRAPHY.

CHAPTER I.

Q. WHERE is the Naze?

A. South of Norway.

Q. What sea lies between Italy and Turkey?

A. The Adriatic Sea.

Q. How are the Alps, the Pyrenees, the Dofrafield, and the Uralian mountains situated?

A. The Pyrenees separate France from Spain; the Dofrafield divide Norway from Sweden; and the Uralian mountains lie north-east of Russia.

Q. Point out the Danube, the Rhine, the Scheldt, the Tagus, and the Seine rivers.

A. See the map of Europe.

Q. In what country is the Tagus river, and into what ocean does it empty itself?

A. Portugal; and falls into the Atlantic Ocean.

Q. Do rivers flow from the sea, or do they rise in the land, and flow into the sea?

A. They rise in the land, and flow into the sea.

Q. Point out the islands of St. Helena, Ceylon, Bombay, and the Falkland Islands.

A. Refer to a map of the world.

Q. Where is the Havannah?

A. On the island of Cuba.

Q. How is Nootka Sound situated?

A. On the west coast near the mouth of the Columbia.

Q. Point out Lima, Quito, Truxillo, St. Jago, Terra-del Fuego, and Chili.

A. Trace them on a map of the world: Look to *South America*.

Q. Where are the gulfs of Finland, Dantzic, and Riga?

A. In the Baltic Sea.

Q. Is Jutland an island?

A. No; it is a *peninsula*.

Q. What is a peninsula?

A. A piece of land almost surrounded by the sea.

Q. Where is the Sound?

A. Between Denmark, Zealand, and Sweden.

Q. What two seas lead to Copenhagen?

A. The Cattegat and the Scaggerack.

Q. What three parts form the kingdom of Denmark.

A. Zealand, Funen, and Jutland, with the adjacent isles.

Q. Where is Cadiz?

A. South-west on the Bay of Cadiz, in the Isle-de-Leon, in Spain.

Q. Point out Brest, Toulon, Marseilles, Jersey, Guernsey, and the Isle of Man.

A. Refer to a map of Europe.

Q. Name the principal islands in the Mediterranean Sea.

A. Repeat them from the map.

CHAPTER II.

Q. In what sea is the Crimea ?

A. The Black Sea.

Q. Where is the whirlpool called the Maël-strom ?*

A. Off the coast of Norway.

Q. In what zone is Great Britain situated ?

A. The north temperate zone.†

Q. Where is the Gulf of Venice ?

A. Between Italy and Turkey.

Q. Where is the Morea ? **A.** In Greece.

Q. How is the Persian Gulf situated ?

A. Between Persia and Arabia.

Q. Opposite to what cape is St. Jago ?

A. Cape Verd in Africa

Q. Do the Sandwich Islands lie in the Eastern or Western hemisphere ?

A. In the Western hemisphere, or Pacific Ocean, opposite California, in North America.

Q. Which are the principal towns in Egypt?

A. Cairo, Alexandria, Rosetta, Damietta, Suez, Nubia, and Abyssinia.

Q. Near what sea does Pekin stand ?

A. The Yellow Sea.

Q. In what empire is Nankin ?

A. China, lying east near the Kian-Ku.

Q. What does the Birman Empire include ?

A. Ava, Pegu, and part of Siam, in India.

---

* If ships happen to be sailing near it, they are drawn in, and dashed to pieces.

† The earth is divided by the small circles into five zones or belts, which may be seen on the globe. The *torrid* zone is the hottest part of the world, and the *frigid* the coldest region.

Q. Is Hindostan a peninsula or an island ?
A. A peninsula.
Q. Is not Bombay on the Malabar coast an island ?   A. Yes.
Q. What chief towns stand on the Ganges ?
A. Bengal, Bahar, Oude, Agra, part of Delhi, &c.
Q. Which is the largest of the West India Islands ?   A. Cuba.
Q. Where does the Nile take its rise ?
A. In Abyssinia.
Q. Into what sea does the Nile empty itself ?
A. The eastern part of the Mediterranean.

CHAPTER III.

Q. WHICH is the largest of the Canary Islands ?
A. Teneriffe.*
Q. What is the chief of New South Wales ?
A. Sydney, in Port Jackson.
Q. Into what sea do the Ganges flow ?
A. The sea of Bengal.
Q. In what ocean are the Sandwich Islands ?
A. In the North Pacific Ocean.
Q. Where is Malta ?
A. In the Mediterranean Sea, south of Sicily.
Q. What sea ports belong to France ?

* The famous peak of Teneriffe is two miles and a half in perpendicular height.

A. Dunkirk, Calais, Boulogne, Dieppe, Cherbourgh, Havre, Saint Malo, Morlaix, Brest, L'Orient, Nantes, Rochelle, Rochfort, Bordeaux; and, in the Mediterranean, Marseilles and Toulon.

Q. In what country are the Lakes of Lagoda and Onega?

A. Russia, near St. Petersburgh.

Q. What seas neither ebb nor flow?

A. The Mediterranean and Baltic Seas.

Q. Is Van Dieman's Land an island?

A. Yes, south of New Holland.

Q. Point out Cape Cormorin.

A. It is the farthest south point of India.

Q. What cluster of islands are those which lie near the equator, in the Indian Ocean.

A. The Mal-divas.

Q. Mention the sea ports on the shores of the Levant.

A. Sidon, Tyre, Acre, or Joppa, and Gaza.

Q. How is Cyprus situated?

A. At the end of the Miditerranean, off the coast of Syria.

Q. Where is Beachy Head?

A. South-east of Sussex.

Q. Where is the Bay of Bengal?

A. East of Hindostan, in India.

Q. On what river is Bagdad? (pronounced *Bagdat.*)

A. On the river Tigris, in Turkey.

Q. Name the chief towns in Hindostan.*

---

* The eastern part of which is called the *Coromandel* coast, and the western the *Malabar.*

A. Calcutta, Madras, Bombay* (an island)
Patna, Benares, Delhi and Surat.

Q. Where does the Indus† rise, and into
what sea does it flow?

A. It rises north-west of Hindostan, near
the source of the Ganges, and, flowing south-
west, falls into the Arabian Sea.

Q. What straits unite the Black Sea and
the sea of Asoph?

A. The straits of Caffa.

Q. Where are the lakes Locarno, Lugana,
and Como?

A. Between Switzerland and Italy.

Q. Where is Spitzbergen?

A. In the North Sea, north of the North
Cape.

Q. Point out, on the map of Europe, Vienna,
Prague, Presburg, Buda, Tokay, and Trieste?

Q. Name the two principal sea-ports of
France on the Mediterranean?

A. Toulon and Marseilles.

Q. Show me on the map of England, the
forty counties, their chief towns, on what river
situated, and how bounded?‡

---

* Calcutta, Madras, and Bombay, are three presidences of the
British possessions in India.

† India takes its name from the appellation given to this
river.

‡ This question need not be answered all at once, but at stated
opportunities.

MISCELLANIES.

CHAPTER I.

Q. NAME the primary planets.

A. Mercury, Venus, the Earth, Mars, Pellas, Ceres, Juno, Jupiter, Saturn, and Georgian, or Georgium Sidus.*

Q. What is a comet?

A. A comet is supposed to be a solid body like the planets.

Q. How do comets appear?

A. Like stars with long illuminated tails.

Q. Have comets any motion ?

A. Comets, like planets, move round the sun; but in very eccentric orbits and irregular periods.

Q. What is a comet's tail supposed to be ?

A. It is supposed to be its atmosphere, either enlightened or set on fire by the sun.

Q. Is the velocity of comets very great ?

A. Yes ; when they are near the sun they move with incredible swiftness.

Q. By what means are the heavenly bodies ; viz. the sun, moon, planets, comets, and stars, kept in their present situation ?

A. By a principle called *gravity*, which is absolutely inseparable from all matter.

* Discovered by Dr. Herschel, March 13th, 1781. In honour of the then King George III. he called it the *Georgium Sidus*.

Q. What is the nature of this principle?

A. It is a principle by which all parts of matter have a constant tendency to approach each other.*

Q. What are fixed stars?

A. They are probably *suns*, conveying light and heat to other worlds.

Q. What other planets have moons besides the earth?

A. Jupiter, Saturn, and Georgian have also moons.

Q. What is the solidity of the earth in comparison with the moon?

A. It is about fifty times as large; but its disc is only thirteen times.

Q. How long would a cannon-ball be reaching the nearest of the planets?

A. More than 1,868,000 years.

Q. What are those stars called which are not visible to the naked eye?

A. Telescopic stars.

Q. What is that broad circle in the heavens, called the Galaxy, or milky way? (Via Lactea.)

A. It is a most extensive stratum of stars.

---

* This tendency, which God has impressed upon matter, pre-serves the great globes which compose our universe in their present places and directions. *Gravity, attraction, weight, centripetal force*, are terms used frequently as synonymous. The phenomena of gravity have been fully explained by Sir I. Newton, and by others who have studied its effects; but its nature or *essence*, and the laws by which it acts, remain yet a secret. Sir I Newton seems to have thought it an *effect* of some external *cause;* perhaps of the action of the sun's heat on some *elastic, rare,* and subtile *fluid.* Dr. Clarke, Halley, Gravesante, and others, consi-der it as a *first and inherent gravity of matter.*

Q. How many stars can be seen by the naked eye in a clear winter's night?

A. Not more than a thousand.*

Q. Are comets supposed to shine by their own native light?

A. Yes, and not by the reflected rays of the sun, as was formerly supposed.

Q. What number of comets is supposed to belong to the planetary system?

A. About one hundred.

Q. Are comets believed to be habitable?

A. No; on account of the very great vicissitudes of heat and cold to which they are subject.†

Q. What is a halo?

A. A meteor in form of a luminous ring round the sun or moon.

CHAPTER II.

Q. Why are the Equator, the Ecliptic, the Meridian, and the Horizon, called *great* circles?

A. Because each of them divides the globe in o two parts.

---

* They seem to be innumerable, which is owing to their strong sparkling, and our looking at them imperfectly or in a confused manner. The number of stars hitherto discovered in both hemispheres, do not exceed 3000. The distance of the nearest fixed star from the earth, is about 32,000,000,000,000 of miles.

† The heat of the comet which appeared in the year 1680, and which will re-appear at the end of 575 years, was estimated by Newton, to have been 2000 times hotter than red hot iron; and he supposed it might retain its heat during a period of twenty thousand years!

Q. What are these two equal parts called?

A. Hemispheres or half globes.

Q. Are there any small circles on the globe?

A. There are eight small circles on each side the equator, and parallel to it, which are called parallels of latitude.

Q. What is their use?

A. To point out the latitude of places with greater accuracy.

Q. What is the length of the day at the equator?

A. The day is always twelve hours long with those who live under the equator.

Q. What is the length of the longest day at the polar circles?

A. About twenty-four hours.

Q. What is the length of the longest day at London.

A. About $16\frac{1}{2}$ hours, which is $4\frac{1}{2}$ hours or 9 half hours longer than at the equator.

Q. How many hours constitute the shortest day at London?

A. About seven hours and a half.

CHAPTER III.

Q. WHAT do you mean by the three estates of the realm?

A. The King,* Lords, and Commons.

Q. In whose hands is the government of the British people vested ?

A. In those of the King and Parliament.

Q. What are the Lords in their collective capacity styled ?

A. The House of Lords.

Q. What the Commons ?

A. The House of Commons.

Q. Who are the Lords spiritual ?

A. The two archbishops and twenty-four bishops of England, and one archbishop and three bishops of Ireland.

Q. Who the Lords temporal ?

A. The nobility; namely, all dukes, marquisses, earls, viscounts, and barons, whether by descent, creation, or election.

Q. How are peers created ?

A. By writ or patent.

Q. How many peers sit in the House of Lords by election ?

A. Forty-four ; namely, sixteen for Scotland and twenty-eight for Ireland.

Q. Of whom is the House of Commons composed ?

A. Of the representatives of the people.

Q. What number of representatives of the

---

* The King, or Queen, if she be the reigning Sovereign, has the sole power of making peace and war ; of concluding all treaties ; of receiving and appointing ambassadors ; of bestowing all civil, military, and naval officers in the kingdom ; of conferring all honours and dignities ; of coining money ; of pardoning offences ; of summoning, adjourning, proroguing, and dissolving Parliament ; of refusing assent to any bill which has passed both Houses of Parliament ; and is the Supreme Head and Governor of the Church of England.

people sit in the Commons' House of Parliament ?

A. Six hundred and fifty-eight.*

Q. What is meant by adjournment of Parliament ?

A. A discontinuance of its sitting for a short time.

Q. What by prorogation ?

A. A discontinuance of the sitting of Parliament from one session to another.

Q. What by dissolution ?

A. The civil death or extinction of Parliament, effected by the King's will on some peculiar occasion.

Q. How many kinds of government are there?

A. Five; namely, Empire, Monarchy, Aristocracy, Democracy, and mixed Government.

Q. What is an Empire ?

A. An assoication of several distinct States.

Q. What is a Monarchy ?

A. A state or nation governed by a king.

Q. What is an Aristocracy ?

A. A state or nation governed by a council or senate, composed of its nobles.

Q. What is a Democracy ?

A. It is that where the rulers are chosen from among the people.

Q. What is a mixed Government ?

A. It is that which partakes of the nature of two or more of the other kinds of government.

* In the House of Commons, forty members must be present to constitute a house; but, in the House of Lords, two peers and the speaker constitute a house.

Questions and Answers

ON

ARITHMETIC.

———

CHAPTER I.

Q. What is Arithmetic, and its use?

A. Arithmetic is the art of computing by numbers. A knowledge of it is absolutely necessary in trade, and even in the common affairs of life.

Q. What are the names of the fundamental rules of arithmetic?

A. The fundamental rules of arithmetic are *Numeration* or *Notation, Addition, Subtraction, Multiplication* and *Division*. Upon these rules all the operations in arithmetic depend; they are therefore called *fundamental.*

Q. What is Numeration?

A. Numeration or Notation teaches us to express numbers by certain characters called figures, and enables us to read and write any sum or number.

Q. How many figures are there?

A. Ten; namely—1, one; 2, two; 3, three; 4, four; 5, five; 6, six; 7, seven; 8, eight, 9, nine; 0, cypher.

Q. What have you to remark of these figures?

A. That nine of them have a certain value when standing alone, and are called significant figures, to distinguish them from the cypher, which, when it stands by itself has no value.

Q. Have not all the figures a different value when they are placed with others ?

A. Yes; for example, when 1 and 2 are placed together they make 12 (twelve); when 2 and 3 are placed together they make 23 (twenty-three); and so on, increasing the value of the left-hand figure in a tenfold proportion.

Q. When has the cypher a value ?

A. When the cypher is put after any figure, the value of the figure is increased tenfold; thus 0 put after 2 makes it 20 (twenty); if two cyphers be added, they make it 200 (two hundred); if three, they make it 2000 (two thousand); every cypher increasing the sum in a tenfold proportion.

Q. What is ADDITION ?

A. Addition is the putting several numbers or sums under each other, so that their total amount may be known by adding them together.

Q. What is SUBTRACTION ?

A. Subtraction teaches us how to take a less number from a greater, and shows the difference or remainder.

Q. What is MULTIPLICATION ?

A. Multiplication is a short way of performing Addition, and on account of its quick dispatch in business, is the most useful rule in arithmetic. By this rule great denominations are brought into small ones; as pounds into shillings, pence or farthings.

Q. Of what does it consist?

A. It consists of three terms, called the *Multiplicand*, the *Multiplier*, and the *Product*.

Q. What do you mean by the Multiplicand?

A. The Multiplicand is the number to be multiplied.

Q. What is the Multiplier?

A. The Multiplier is the number by which the work is to be performed, and is placed under the Multiplicand.

Q. What is the Product?

A. The Product is the number produced by multiplying, and is called the Answer.

Q. What is DIVISION?

A. Division is a short way of performing Subtraction, and shows how many times one number or sum is contained in another. By this rule small denominations are brought into greater; as farthings into pence, shillings or pounds.

Q. What are the terms made use of in Division?

A. These three; namely, the *Dividend*, the *Divisor*, and the *Quotient*.

Q. What is the Dividend?

A. The Dividend is the number required to be divided.

Q. What is the Divisor?

A. The Divisor is the number by which we divide, or perform the work.

Q. What is the Quotient?

A. The Quotient is the Answer to the work, showing how often the Divisor is contained in the Dividend.

BOOK-KEEPING.

MERCHANTS generally keep their books, or mercantile accounts, by *double entry ;* and retail dealers (under the class of Tradesmen,) by *single entry*.

In single entry two books only are required ; namely, the day-book and the ledger.

The day-book represents, in the first instance, the owner's property; and afterwards the daily occurrences of his dealings with others.

The ledger collects the dispersed accounts, and arranges them on the Dr. and Cr. side as the transactions occur.

To understand clearly the nature of single entry, the following rule must be carefully observed :—

The person who receives an article is Dr. for that article ; and the person of whom any thing is received, whether cash or goods, is Cr. for that cash, or those goods.

On the Dr. side or page of the ledger stands all that has been bought of you, or you have lent on credit : on the Cr. side the cash, &c. you have received ; and the difference of the two opposite accounts shows the balance.

ABBREVIATIONS.

A.B. or B.A. (Artium Baccalaureus) *Bachelor of Arts.*

A. C. (Ante Christum) *before Christ.*

A. D. (Anno Domini) *in the year of our Lord.*

A. M. (Artium Magister) *Master of Arts.*

A. M. (Anno Mundi) *in the year of the world.*

A. M. (Ante Meridiem) *before noon.*

Bart. *Baronet.*

D.D. (Divinitatis Doctor) *Doctor of Divinity.*

I. H. S. (Jesus Hominum Salvator) *Jesus the Saviour of mankind.*

J. U. D. (Juris Utriusque Doctor) *Doctor of Laws.*

LL.D. (Legum Doctor) *Doctor of the Canon and Civil Law.*

M. A. *Master of Arts.*

M. D. (Medicinæ Doctor) *Doctor of Medicine. Doctor of Physic.*

Mem. (Memento) *remember.*

M. S. (Memoriæ Sacrum) *sacred to memory.*

Per cent. (per centum) *by the hundred.*

P. M. (Post meridiem) *afternoon.*

S. T. P. (Sacræ Theologiæ Professor) *Professor of Theology.*

Ult. (Ultimo) *the last.*

Explanation

OF SOME OF THE

CHIEF TERMS AND PHRASES

IN COMMON USE.

———◆———

Alias, otherwise.

Alibi, elsewere.

Bona fide, in reality.

Compos mentis, in one's senses.

Dei gratia, by the grace of God.

Errata, errors in print, &c.

Ex-king, ex-minister, the late king, or the late minister.

Ex-parte, on the part of, or on one side.

Fac simile, a close imitation.

Felo de se, self-murderer.

Finis, the end.

Gratis, for nothing

Ibid or *ibidem*, in the same place.

Id est, (i. e.) that is.

In propria personæ, in person.

In terrorem, as a warning.

In statu quo, in the former state.

Item, also.

Memento mori, remember death.

Multum in parvo, a great deal in a small compass.

Ne plus ultra, no farther, or to the utmost extent.

Non compos mentis, out of one's senses.

O tempora ! O mores ! O the times, O the manners.

Onus, burden.

Prima facia, on the first appearance of a thing.

Pro and con, for and against.

Pro bono publico, for the public benefit.

Pro forma, for form's sake.

Pro tempore, for the time.

Resurgam, I shall rise again.

Rex, the king.

Regina, the queen.

Scandalum magnatum, scandal against the nobility.

Senatum, in regular order.

Sine die, without mentioning any particular day.

Sine qua non, indispensable requisite or condition.

Sub-pœna, a writ threatening a penalty in case of refusal or disobedience to legal authority.

Summum bonum, greatest good.

Vade mecum, constant companion.

Veluti in speculum, as in a looking glass.

Versus, against.

Vice versa, the reverse.

Vide, see.

Vivunt rex et regina, long live the king and queen.

Utile dulci, utility with pleasure.

COMMERCIAL TERMS,*

ALPHABETICALLY ARRANGED.

———•———

Agent. One authorized to act for another.

Acceptor. He who writes his name on a bill and undertakes to pay the same.

Bills of exchange. A written order for payment of money.†

Bills of parcels. An account rendered by the seller to the buyer, containing an account of the goods bought.

Bond. A deed or obligation, by which a person binds himself to pay a certain sum of money.

Cheque A draft on a banker, ordering payment of a sum of money.

Cocket. A custom house warrant, given on the entry of goods, to show that they have paid duty.

Credit side. The right-hand side of an account.

Days of grace. A certain number of days allowed for the payment of a bill, after the term is expired.

Debit side. The left-hand side of an account.

---

* These may be learned *interrogatively*, if it be thought proper.

† The *drawer* is the person who writes the order : the *acceptor* signs his name for the payment of it.

Discount. An allowance made for prompt or immediate payment.

Dividend. A share of any profit, or money vested in the funds, &c.

Docket A short memorandum or summary, affixed to larger papers.*

Draft. A bill or cheque, by which one person draws for money on another; also an allowance deducted from the original weight of goods.

Draw-back. An allowance of premium for the exportation of goods.

Drawer. He who makes a bill of exchange.

Drawee. He upon whom a bill of exchange is drawn.

Endorser. He that writes his name on the back of a bill or note.

Errors excepted. Are words placed at the bottom of an account to claim allowance for omissions or over charges.

Endorsement. The putting one's name on the back of a bill.

Freight. The goods which a ship carries; also the money paid for their conveyance.

Gross weight. The whole weight of goods, *including* casks, chests, bags, baskets, &c.

Instant. This month.

Insolvent. One who is unable to pay his debts.

Instalments. Payments on a sum of money, in certain proportions, and at stipulated times.

Letters of advice. A letter giving notice of any transaction.

* *Striking a docket,* is when a creditor gives bond to the Lord Chancellor, proving his debtor to be a bankrupt.

Letters of attorney or power of attorney. A writing which empowers one person to act for another.

Letter of credit. A letter by which one person can receive money on the credit of another.

Liquidation. The concluding or winding up of a business, as paying and receiving all debts, &c.

Maximum. The highest price of any article.

Minimum. The lowest price of any article.

Net, or net weight. The exact weight of any large commodity, after all deductions have been made.

Noting. The act of a notary* when a bill is not duly honoured or paid.

Permit. A licence or warrant for the passing or selling of goods, which have paid duty to government.

Protest. A paper made out by a notary public, declaring a bill to have been refused payment or acceptance.

Receipt. A written acknowledgment of having received a sum of money.

Remittance. Cash forwarded from one person or place to another.

Salary. Yearly wages paid to a teacher, clerk, &c. for services rendered to his employer.

Tally. A cleft piece of wood to score an account upon.

Tare. An allowance for the weight of package.

---

* A notary public is one duly appointed to attend deeds and other writings; and also to note or protest bills of exchange, drafts or notes, when unpaid or returned.

Tret. An allowance for waste, dust, &c. not usually adopted now in the weighing of goods; nor is the word *cloff* mentioned, but *draft*, which is an allowance made for the turn of the scale. *Tret*, formerly, was a deduction of 4lb. in every 104lb. and *cloff*, 2lb. in every 3 cwt.

Tender. An offer to pay a debt.

Tonnage. Certain duties imposed on goods.

Ullage. What a cask wants of being full.

Ultimo. The last month.

Usance. A certain period after date.

Usury. The charge of interest beyond five per cent.

Underwriter. A person who insures ships, cargoes, or other risks, which is performed by writing his name under a policy of insurance.

FIGURES AND NUMBERS.

	Arabic.	Roman.		Arabic.	Roman.
One	1	I	Twenty-one	21	XXI
Two	2	II	Twenty-five	25	XXV
Three	3	III	Thirty	30	XXX
Four	4	IV	Forty	40	XL
Five	5	V	Fifty	50	L
Six	6	VI	Sixty	60	LX
Seven	7	VII	Seventy	70	LXX
Eight	8	VIII	Eighty	80	LXXX
Nine	9	IX	Ninety	90	XC
Ten	10	X	One Hundred	100	C
Eleven	11	XI	Two Hundred	200	CC
Twelve	12	XII	Three Hundred	300	CCC
Thirteen	13	XIII	Four Hundred	400	CCCC
Fourteen	14	XIV	Five Hundred	500	D
Fifteen	15	XV	Six Hundred	600	DC
Sixteen	16	XVI	Seven Hundred	700	DCC
Seventeen	17	XVII	Eight Hundred	800	DCCC
Eighteen	18	XVIII	Nine Hundred	900	DCCCC
Nineteen	19	XIX	One Thousand	1000	M
Twenty	20	XX	1837		M.DCCC.XXXVII

THE END.

www.ingramcontent.com/pod-product-compliance
Lightning Source LLC
Chambersburg PA
CBHW081521040426
42447CB00013B/3292